Living The Life
—— OF ——
WORSHIP

Rev. J.C. Banda

Living the Life of Worship
© Rev. J.C. Banda 2025

All rights reserved. No part of this publication may be reproduced, stored in a retrieval system, or transmitted, in any form or by any means—electronic, mechanical, photocopying, recording, or otherwise—without the prior written permission of the publisher, except in the case of brief quotations embodied in critical articles or reviews.

Scripture quotations, unless otherwise indicated, are taken from the Holy Bible, New International Version®, NIV®. Copyright © 1973, 1978, 1984, 2011 by Biblica, Inc.™ Used by permission. All rights reserved worldwide.

Scripture quotations marked KJV are taken from the Holy Bible, King James Version, Public Domain.

ISBN 978-1-7385422-9-1

Printed and bound in the United Kingdom

Published by Rev. J.C. Banda

An Explanation of an Anchor

Biblical meaning of an anchor:
STRENGTH AND STEADFASTNESS

Strength:

Trusting in the Lord as our true source of strength
(Joshua 1:9)

Steadfastness:

To be constant, faithful, loyal, or unwavering
in faith to God
(James 1:12; Hebrews 10:23)

Table of Contents

Dedication 7

Acknowledgements 9

Introduction 11

1 - The One God to Be Worshipped is Holy 19

2 - The Role of the Bible in Worship Life 27

3 - Spiritual and Physical Balanced Diet 33

4 - True Worship in Life 49

5 - The People's Divine Experiences of the Triune God 69

References 83

Dedication

This book on "Living the Life of Worship" is dedicated to my family members and all people who feel the passion to pray seriously for themselves and others, to make use of the time given to them graciously by God to be better people spiritually and morally during this challenging time we are living in.

Social challenges are on the rise like unemployment; marriage instability resulting in divorces; single family parenting; anti-social behaviour among children who are supposed to be preparing themselves to be responsible leaders of nations in adulthood by acquiring good wholesome education with skills that bring about productivity; drug abuse, use of dark arts by youths and adults to enrich themselves; corruption which is always a means of acquiring wealth through immoral ways while disadvantaging the diligent citizens by dragging them into poverty and some immoral ways of living; political instability, atheism and unnecessary despotic wars that take the lives of many innocent babies, youths and adults whose owner is none other than God who created them in His own image. "How does God feel in such social situations?" This is the author's rhetorical question.

Acknowledgements

My prayerful spouse, Mavis Banda with the help of God, has inspired me massively to the extent of writing this book. She, being an active participant in prayer-line devotions which she and Mrs Marylyn Maiwasha as an administrator appointed by her, got registered in the United States of America on the 4th of March 2014 and established it to use for the United Methodist Church on Sunday morning devotions in the United Kingdom, opened my eyes to a lot of possibilities.

This section prayer group grew to include members of other Christian denominations. The worshippers decided to have morning devotions every morning from 05:00hrs to 07:00hrs every day, through the telephone free conference calls. Other worship activities are carried out at various times by those who are free to participate from 09:00hrs to 10:00hrs, 12:00hrs to 13:00hrs, 15:00hrs to 16:00hrs, 21:00hrs to 22:00hrs and at midnight. This is done in the comfort of their homes. Volunteer interdenominational preachers, teachers of the word of God, and group discussions on social matters and intercessors who intercede for different worldwide social situations volunteer to play their roles while giving reverence and glory to God for whom we were all created to obey and

worship. From this telephone free conference prayer-line group which the author attends quietly but eagerly and attentively has greatly been enriching spiritually and encouraging worshippers to travel this journey of faith with hope of a better future on earth and in heaven for believers in the Triune God through faith in Jesus, His perfect revelation to mankind for our salvation from sin and eternal death *(John 3:16)*.

Also, to be acknowledged are family members in the locality with whom the author discussed religious and social matters like Dr. H.H. Banda, Mrs. T. Chiwara and Mr. S. Banda who took the responsibility of creating a typed script of the book with amazing dedication for the book to reach the eager waiting readers for their spiritual nourishment intellectual growth and new insights for spiritual and moral amelioration.

Introduction

In family life, living in intimate relationships is a joyous practice physically, psychologically, and spiritually. It is in such a relationship that children who are blessings from God to us in the family and in the society, learn a lot of things about family life in general. They quickly know how to live humanly and responsibly by learning from the disciplined parents who uphold general social values to live well with others in the society.

Disciplined children, in most cases, end up being responsible, loving, respectful and caring adults of integrity. However, some of them might become social misfits because of adopting negative attitudes against the social norms and values. Environments, peer anti-social groups, unruly adult practices, parental negligence of child training and supervision, contribute to the anti-social activities of children in the society.

The church is supposed to be taken as a much larger family unit of believers made up of parents and their children who refer to God as their Father on whom they depend and should obey for their uprightness, spiritually and morally since He is holy. If we live in harmony with God, peace with Him and fellow people ensues. To disobey the Father in heaven is to rebel against Him. This rebellion results in indiscipline among people who seek to do things that please them though contrary to the will of God, their heavenly Father whom they ought to believe in or trust.

Fighting against God in words and deeds, is sinning against Him. Sin has some negative results spiritually, morally and practically which might be interpreted as God's punishment. If the perpetrators of sin do not repent from their practices till death strikes, they miss the gracious time of repentance of sinners and forgiveness of sins after death. What awaits the resurrected people from the dead is the judgement of the righteous and just God who judges according to what the people did when they were still living on earth *(Matthew 25:31-46)*. Paul gives a serious warning to people which they should take heed of, in his letter to the *Romans 6:23*, where he says, *"For the wages of sin is death, but the gift of God is eternal life in Christ Jesus our Lord."* Self-control as a Christian virtue, helps us to refrain from committing sins which cut our relationship with God spiritually and lead us, mortal beings into a rebellion against God who is immortal and invincible. Ultimately this sin leads to eternal death after the death that we will all experience on earth if not forgiven by God through our penitence on earth. God loves all human beings hence all human beings enjoy His unmerited grace. By His grace, we live, work, have possessions, prosper economically, regardless of our spiritual status but the time will come for us to give accounts of what we have done on earth, on which God's judgement will be based. God loves all the people and urges them to live well but hates the sinful activities they do which corrupt them spiritually and morally.

Living a virtuous life is what is expected of us all. The two greatest commandments are mentioned in their order in *Matthew 22:36-40* and they are to be seriously observed for they summarise the will of God to be followed according to the Christian belief. Jesus presented what worshipping God entails thus: *"Love the Lord your God with all your heart and with all your soul and with all your mind."* This is the first and greatest commandment and the second is like it: *"Love your neighbour as yourself."* The love of God is evidenced by whole-hearted devotion to God coupled with loving other people as we love ourselves.

The relationship to be observed by believers in God are the vertical relationship with God and the horizontal one with fellow human beings to please God. Violation of any of the two commandments renders us sinners. However, the merciful God we worship is ready to forgive the remorseful penitent sinners and build up the broken relationship between Him and the perpetrator of sins. This is what we learn from Jesus' parable of the Prodigal Son found in the Gospel according to *Luke 15:11-31*.

The Christians who profess to know the Triune God, should love God Himself by obeying or having faith in Him in order to have a spiritual communion with Him. God is to be worshipped with reverence because of what He is and what He does in the universe for our existence. He is the foundation of life without whose assistance we cannot survive. As for us, human beings, we should try our best to live the worship life in thought, word and deed to live in harmony with Him.

Lest we forget in this busy and entertaining world, where time is flying so fast and our minds left boggled, in the prioritisation of what to do first and last, we should remember what lies at the end of this known time. God's judgement will ultimately be based on our choices of what to do and what not to do. Wrong choices that lead to wrong deeds that are abominable to God, are punishable whereas the righteous and just ones are rewardable by the righteous and just God in His final judgement. Putting our faith into practice during the short period of our existence on earth, is very significant for a future life. When soul and body are still intact that is the convenient time to prepare for eternal life.

This book aims at encouraging people to see by faith, though faintly, what lies beyond the spiritual horizon when we do not believe God's truth about our liberation from sin as canonised in the Bible about life on earth, its end on earth and the miraculous resurrection of the dead. This event of the resurrection is logically followed by the rewarding of the saved people from the second and eternal death. The condemned ones will eternally perish as expressed in the Bible *(John 3:16)*. Let us truly repent and adhere to our faith in Jesus to hope for living in eternity with the Lord.

Christians testify what takes place when people have faith in God through Jesus Christ in songs and hymns like the hymn that follows:

The United Methodist Church Shona Hymn "Ngerutendo Rukuru"

Key: Doh is A - Tune "The Old Time Religion"

Ngerutendo rukuru,
By the great faith,

Ngerutendo rukuru,
By the great faith,

Ngerutendo rukuru,
By the great faith,

Vanhu vanopona ndirwo,
People are saved by it,

Rwakanakira Daniel, x3
It was good for Daniel,

Saka rwakandinakira,
That is why it is good for me,

Rwakanakira Pauro, x3
It was good for Paul,

Rwakanakira Peter,
It was good for Peter,

Rwakanakira Dorka,
It was good for Dorcas,

Rwakanakira Ruthi,
It was good for Ruth,

Rwakanditenderudza,
It converted me,

Rwakandipa chisepe,
It gave me love,

Rwakandipa rukundo,
It gave me victory,

Rwakandipa kuziva,
It gave me knowledge,

Rwakandipa ungwaru,
It gave me wisdom,

Rwakandipa upenyu
It gave me life,

Rwakandipa rufaro,
It gave me joy,

Runondi tungamira,
It guides me,

Runondi pfawisisa,
It makes me humble,

Runondikwidza kudenga,
It takes me to heaven,

The Old Time Religion

Refrain
Give me that old time religion
Give me that old time religion
Give me that old time religion,
   It is good enough for me.

1. It was good for Paul and Silas,
   It was good for Paul and Silas,
   It was good for Paul and Silas,
      It is good enough for me.

Refrain

2. It was good for the Hebrew children,
   It was good for the Hebrew children,
   It was good for the Hebrew children,
      It is good enough for me.

Refrain

3. It was good for our mothers,
   It was good for our mothers,
   It was good for our mothers,
      It is good enough for me.

Refrain

4. Makes me love everybody,
Makes me love everybody,
Makes me love everybody,
It is good enough for me.

Refrain

The Biblical Characters Who Lived the Life of Worship

Jesus Christ, the Son of God is the highest role model of Christians' spirituality and morality because He was truly God and truly man physically through incarnation. He originally was known as the Word then became a man like us for our sake through birth by the virgin Mary *(John 1:1-4; Matthew 1:18-25; Luke 1:26-38; Luke 2:1-21)*. The others in the Old Testament were Noah, Abraham, Jacob, Joseph, Moses, Joshua, Deborah, David and the prophets. In the New Testament there were: John the Baptist, Mary the mother of Jesus, the disciples of Jesus but Judas Iscariot in the end performed below the mark when he betrayed the Lord, the apostles amongst whom were Paul and Dorcas to mention a few who lived the life of worship to stay connected to God through obedience. From these, people have learnt a lot of things that have transformed them spiritually and morally through their lives, teachings, preaching, the books and letters they wrote to the churches.

CHAPTER ONE

The One God to Be Worshipped is Holy

To monotheist believers (believers in one God) like the Jews and the Trinitarian monotheistic Christian believers (believers in three Persons in One God) who believe in God the Father, God the Son and God the Holy Spirit, interpret worship as giving worthiness to God for what He is and what He does to people and things He created. God is Almighty, present everywhere, all knowing and the Sovereign Ruler. Such belief leads the believers to live the life of worship daily. They create a culture of living in honour or reverence to God or they adopt the attitude of loving God whole-heartedly as is said in *Matthew 22:37*.

The book of wisdom, the Proverbs, talks about the attitude of fearing God which is a deep feeling that the transcendent God is Holy, adorable, gracious and there is no one like Him in heaven and on earth. He loves all the people He created in His image but hates and punishes sinfulness. Fearing God is to have a deep reverence and love for the Lord as is said by King Solomon in *Proverbs 1:7*, *"The fear of the Lord is the beginning of knowledge, but fools despise wisdom and instruction."* In *Proverbs 3:7* King Solomon said, *"Do not be wise in your eyes, fear the Lord and shun evil."* These sayings of King Solomon are inspired by God Himself to help people to acknowledge Him as the source of wisdom which is needed for their welfare and safety where sins of different types are prevalent universally. Living in harmony and joy with God through faith and deeds is to be aimed at by believers in God's Kingdom that has been established on earth to be entered by believers in God through faith in Jesus and by God's grace. God takes the initiative to reveal Himself to the people through the created things and His only begotten Son, Jesus Christ the only hope of our salvation from sin and eternal death *(John 3:16; Romans 1:18-32; 2:1-16)*.

Worship is not done in the church building or among the congregation of Christian believers only but spreads out of the sanctuaries and corporate worship. Believers can worship in groups or individually where and when they enjoy quality time or special time to pray, sing and read the scriptures and reflect on them for spiritual nourishment and growth. Worship can be done in the homes by having evening prayers, singing hymns of praises and thanksgiving for what God is and what He does to us day by day. Christians as the body of Jesus, should come together and worship at least once a week in the church or sanctuary where they can spiritually and psychologically experience the presence of God as they adore Him. It is through this communion with God our Lord and Saviour that we can be strengthened spiritually and morally through sermons, teachings, testimonies, singing and prayers.

After the Sunday service, worship goes on outside the churches where we translate our faith into action through evangelism, righteousness and charity. People to be converted should see our good deeds for them to affirm the goodness of worshipping God. Jesus, in His sermon on the mount said, "In the same way, let your light shine before others, that they may see your good deeds and glorify your Father in heaven *(Matthew 5:16)*. The light of God shines in believers through the good things they do in the world spiritually, morally, intellectually, physically, socially and materially through enlightenment and transformation for the better. Wisdom is like hidden treasure which has to be sought tirelessly and when it is found great joy ensues. King Solomon in *Proverbs 9:10-12* says, *"The fear of God is the beginning of wisdom and knowledge of the Holy One is understanding. For through wisdom your days will be many, and years will be added to your life. If you are wise, your wisdom will reward you; if you are a mocker, you alone will suffer."* The moral principles should be observed in our social interactions. When we behave responsibly and we are dependable we serve God and the people faithfully. This is how we can avert sinfulness and live righteously in light of God's will. Acting responsibly is part of worship. We fear to behave irresponsibly as the adopted children of God who aim at becoming upright in thought, word and deed. Any wrong deed done to our neighbour, should be met with remorse and repentance, to be forgiven by God who is ready to forgive anyone who repents wholeheartedly.

Every day of the year, believers are supposed to be in the attitude of worshipping God to placate Him and to live safely and peacefully with our neighbours for that is the will of God for us. By so doing we bear the fruits of the Spirit which are: love, joy, peace, patience, goodness, faithfulness, gentleness and self-control mentioned by the Apostle Paul in *Galatians 5:22-26*. Adopting the worship living is in line with what Jesus used to do when He was living on earth. The life of Jesus as the Son of God is a high spiritual and moral norm which ought to be emulated and imitated by the born-again Christians who are the co-heirs of Jesus Christ, the perfect revelation of God the Father to the humanity. The disciples and the apostles who were inspired by the Holy Spirit adopted the practices of Jesus' worshipping of God the Father privately and publicly. Today Christians who are also the disciples, from the Latin word 'discipulus,' meaning a learner and the plural 'discipuli' meaning learners. The church will always learn from Jesus the Good News to all the people in the world. The church as the apostles still learns from Jesus who sent them into the world to preach and teach the word of God in order to make the disciples of Jesus Himself as alluded to in the Gospel according to *Matthew 28:18-20*.

What Jesus taught through His life, teachings and preaching became our heritage to nourish our life spiritually and morally for us to continue to be the salt and light of the world. While living in the *'chronos'* time which is the general time that can be calculated, the *'kyros'* time, quality or special time should be created by the committed believer in the true, living God, to be in communion with Him when and where we can dialogue with Him spiritually through prayers, singing and reflecting on the word of God in the Bible. Nothing has been hidden from us by God for our salvation from sin and eternal death. Obedience is a sign of humility and commitment to what has been revealed to us by God whose unconditional love 'agape' reaches us all. However, to be grateful or ungrateful is our choice with consequences, of course, because God is righteous and just. Good deeds are rewardable but bad ones are punishable. In this quality time with God our Father, we should be humble, respectful, and grateful to Him and listen to what He says to us individually and collectively. The Holy Spirit is at work trying to convict us of our sins which we should confess and repent from, to be in communion with God the Father.

In response, God will guide and encourage us to travel the journey of faith that leads to eternity by God's grace. Faith in God makes us hope for things He promises us to have and experience in the new life to come. God is immutable in that He fulfils what He promises, as He is faithful to Himself. Gracious time for us, to make choices acceptable to God is now, when the soul and body are intact. Let us sow and reap in faith and experience the amazing grace of God here on earth and hereafter in eternity. Let us be faithful messengers of the Lord by saying or singing a hymn like, "Look and live."

Look and Live

1. Look and live, my brother live
Look at Jesus now and live
'Tis recorded in His word, Hallelujah!
It is only that you look and live.

2. I've a message full of love, Hallelujah!
A message O my friend, for you.
'Tis a message from above, Hallelujah!
Jesus said it, and I know 'tis true (Refrain)

3. Life is offered unto you, Hallelujah!
Eternal life your soul shall have.
If you'll look to Him. Hallelujah!
Look to Jesus, who alone can save (Refrain)

4. I will tell you how I came, Hallelujah!
To Jesus when He made me whole.
'T was believing on His name Hallelujah!
I trusted and He saved my soul (Refrain)

Source: "One Lord, One Faith, One Baptism: an African American ecumenical hymnal #412, author, W.A. Ogden.

On the next page is the same hymn sung in the Shona Language in Zimbabwe, in the United Methodist Church.

Hymn 161

Ndinouya NemaSoko
Doh is G - Tune: Look and Live

1. Ndinouya nemasoko erudo,
   Masoko akakomba edi,
   Kuti Baba wakatida zvikuru,
   Anofara kuponesa tese.

Korusi
Munangise hama dzangu,
Muna Muponesi zvino,
Uyo anotenda iye apone,
Munangisei, hama dzangu mwese.

2. Ndinouya nemasoko kunemwi,
   Masoko akanaka enyu,
   Kuti Kristu, wakafira vatadzi,
   Munangise anomuponesa.

3. Jesu Kristu wakandisunungura,
   Upenyu hwake wakandipa,
   Ndakatenda izwi rake mumwoyo,
   Mweya wangu wakapona ndiye.

4. Nhasi, kuti uchimunangisisa,
   Mumwoyo nekufunga kwese,
   Uchiuya kuna iye nerudo,
   Jesu Kristu anokuponesa.

5. Kuti uchiramba Jesu M'ponesi,
   Nerudo rwake rwakadai,
   Ungapona senyi musi mukuru,
   Musi anotonga vanhu vese?

Christian believers are sojourners in the world. The letter to the *Hebrews 13:14-16* says, *"For here we do not have an enduring city, but we are looking for the city that is to come. Through Jesus, therefore, let us continually offer to God a sacrifice of praise - the fruit of lips that openly profess his name and do not forget to do good and to share with others, for with such sacrifices God is pleased."*

In the *'chronos'* time, let us work for our welfare and safety with the help of God. We should uphold our Christian norms and values in life that will enable us to inherit eternal life through faith in Jesus and by God's grace *(John 3:16)*. The world is endowed with great wealth which we can have for our good. However, the acquisition of some of this wealth should not drive us away from God who gave it to us to use unselfishly of course. Focusing on Jesus as we toil on earth for our existence, will help the Christian believers act responsibly to preserve Christian norms and values even under tempting situations. Wealth can easily become a great temptation that can dampen our faith to the extent of becoming apostatic, proud, selfish, corrupt, or immoral. The Apostle Paul warns the Christians against conformity to the world. He said, *"Do not conform to the pattern of this world, but be transformed by the renewing of your mind. Then you will be able to test and approve what God's will is - His good, pleasing and perfect will." (Romans 12:2).*

The Christian spiritual and moral standards are very high but they should be aimed at always because they are necessary in our final process of spiritual sanctification, after the prevenient and justifying gracious processes towards the miraculous perfection, through faith in Jesus and by God's grace. Jesus is perfect whereas we are imperfect. Faith in God's grace paradoxically makes the imperfect, perfect to inherit eternal life. We cannot be perfect on our own for we all fall short of God's glory *(Romans 3: 23-24)*. We cannot be saved through the good deeds we do without faith in God through Jesus *(Ephesians 2: 8-10)*. As we believe in Jesus, we should try our best to live righteously. Though our best is not good enough to merit salvation, we can be saved by the unmerited grace of God through the faith in Jesus we uphold.

CHAPTER TWO

The Role of the Bible in Worship Life

The Bible, *'Ta Biblia'* in Greek which means, 'The Books,' is a collection of thirty-nine books in the Old Testament and twenty-seven in the New Testament, all of which are God-inspired for our spirituality and morality *(2 Timothy 3:16-17)*. This Bible is the canonised revelation of the Triune God. It contains the *'Missio Dei'* Latin for 'Mission of God,' which contains the creation of heaven and earth, the fall of man to be saved through the law or commandments to be obeyed, restoration of the lost or fallen people and redemption of the sinners through the death of Jesus Christ on the cross.

What follows *'Missio Dei'* is the *'Missio Ecclesia'* meaning the 'Mission of the Church' initiated by Jesus Christ after His resurrection from the dead through His Great Commission to His disciples in *Matthew 28:18-20* when Jesus said, *"All authority in heaven and on earth has been given to me. Therefore, go and make disciples of all nations, baptising them in the name of the Father and of the Son and of the Holy Spirit, and teaching them to obey everything I have commanded you. And surely, I am with you always, to the very end of the age."*

In *Luke 4:18-19* Jesus declared His mission in the world by saying, *"The Spirit of the Lord is in me,"* because he has anointed me to proclaim freedom for the prisoners and recovery of sight for the blind, to set the oppressed free, to proclaim the year of the Lord's favour."* Teaching and preaching the word of God became the mission of the church in order to make the disciples of Jesus and as a means of salvation through faith of the converts and by God's grace. The Bible carries the history of humanity through the death of Jesus on the cross to redeem humanity from sin and eternal death. This is the good salvation news to all human beings as alluded to in *John 3:16*. It is now the noble responsibility of the church to spread the good news of Jesus to all nations for repentance for the forgiveness of our sins by God through faith in Jesus. Time is flying and our time on earth is short and yet people of all nations need to hear and understand this truthful word of salvation. When the body and soul are still intact, we live during the unmerited period of grace to prepare spiritually and morally for the day of our departure from the earth to be acceptable by our Lord hereafter, to live another life eternally.

The Bible contains all that we need to know about our purpose of living in the world, how to live responsibly to the joy of God and safety and comfort of oneself and others on earth. Obedience or faith is required of us as humble citizens of the kingdom of God on earth. Biblical interpretations devoid of human misinterpretations present the Bible as an instrument of liberation spiritually, mentally, morally and socially as it is meant to be.

Some of the people tend to be impervious to the biblical facts because of how the Bible was used or is still used by deceitful preachers bent on misleading congregations for their own benefit. This is misuse of the Bible as an object. This is why there is need to defend the faith of the church. The church has been battling with heresies in the church that misdirect the believers and converts. As long as the universal tempter - the devil, is among us to mislead people or to be rebellious against God, the church will need to take their positions to defend their faith in God through Jesus for people to be saved from sin and eternal death. Christians should preach and teach through the word of God and their deeds. Serving God and people demands sacrifice in many aspects of life by applying endurance, tolerance, patience, faith and agapeic love in order to give services to people indiscriminately.

The Bible abounds in teaching on the Triune God, what He did, does and will eternally do in the second life for the saved ones. The disciples and apostles contributed many teachings on spirituality and morality in the person's lifestyle. Such teachings help to transform the minds of believers to adopt high standards of living spiritually and morally according to the will of God. As the apostle Paul says in *Romans 10:17* that faith comes from hearing the message, and the message is heard through hearing the word about Christ. Reading the Bible with understanding and listening to the proclamation of the word of God help the listeners to rise to a higher level of faith. This faith is a supernatural gift of God as alluded to in *Acts 11:18* and *2 Timothy 2:25*; *Ephesians 2:8-9*.

The Significance of Faith in the Worship Life

Faith or belief in God helps a believer to hunger and thirst after righteousness which can be satisfied by God who draws close to those who are in search of spiritual satisfaction that transforms attitudes and behaviour of believers. The two sidedness of faith is very significant to those who are humble and ready to listen to what God says in the Bible and through personal experiences in life as they keep on worshipping God.

Some divine insights throw light on obscure Bible verses for better understanding and guidance in moving forward in faith against all odds, for our own salvation and for the joy of God. As faith was given to our predecessors in the Christian belief, it is given to all who trust in God or who are humble before Him. The concealed truth about God and what He does to us, are exposed through faith which is the link between God and worshippers living in communion. Faith was experienced by great people recorded in the Bible like Noah, Abraham, Isaac, Jacob, Joseph, Moses, Joshua, the prophets, Jesus, the disciples, and apostles of Jesus who handed over the tradition to the church which is made up of the people called out of the world by God under the leadership of Jesus Christ to serve God Himself and the world for the people's salvation from sin and eternal death. Those who hear and accept the proclaimed word of God are referred to as blessed people by Jesus in His sermon on the mount in *Matthew 5:1-12*. Those who accept Jesus as their personal saviour and are baptised in the name of God, the Son and the Holy Spirit are called God's children by adoption and coheirs with Jesus Christ *(John 1:12-13; Romans 8:17)*. It is interesting and encouraging to learn from the letter to the Hebrews Chapters 11 and 12 on faith and God's discipline to His children as He leads them to eternity. In His holiness and love, God disciplines His children to show them the seriousness and goodness of obeying Him to achieve the great things awaiting them in the life to come.

There are many bad things that are to be avoided in being a well-disciplined person like hatred, covetousness, plots, corruption, murder, promiscuity, stealing, oppression, greed, pride, tribalism, racism, nepotism, avarice among other vices. Such social practices adversely affect the doers and others in the society to the extent of offending God our Maker and Owner. Where such practices are prevalent, people live under unnecessary life-threatening situations that dehumanise them and lead them to loss of dignity, possessions and even the precious God-given gift of life.

There is need for the reawakening of human minds that comes by self-assessments of the personal attitudes and behaviour, towards oneself and others in the society. The goal for such a practice is to find out what is good for the greatest number of people to avert selfishness, bigotry, and ruthlessness in any society. For the Christians, Love 'Agape' as interpreted in Greek is a strong ethical principle to be applied in serving God and the people. God Himself is known as *LOVE*. The apostle John in his first letter to believers says, *"And so for us. God is love. Whoever lives in love lives in God, and God in them. This is how love is made complete among us so that we will have confidence on the day of judgement. In this world we are like Jesus." (1 John 4:16-17)*.

The agape love is the love that God loves us with. It is unconditional and knows no bounds. In *Matthew 5:43-45*, Jesus urges us to imitate God by saying these words to the listeners: *"You heard that it was said, 'Love your neighbour and hate your enemy. But I tell you, love your enemies and pray for those who persecute you, that you may be children of your Father in heaven."* He causes the sun to rise on the evil and good, and sends rain on the righteous and the unrighteous. This kind of living is part of the worship life that should be lived daily. Here the moral standard is very high for us human beings but God expects us to live according to His will. Generally human will is contrary to God's will. For us to be humble and selfless, we must abandon our own wrong will to do God's will which is righteous and just. With God's help that kind of living is possible though difficult to follow.

God is wholly other in nature or supernaturally unique. Only a few human characteristics resemble His. As born-again Christians, we must capitalise on the goodness realised through faith, to be aligned to God's will for our good and that of others who may be of other beliefs. According to God's plan for people's existence, people must co-exist upholding the social principle of interdependence. All people are God's images hence all of them should be reached with the word of God for God Himself loves them to be His eternally, provided they obey Him for salvation is through faith in Jesus and by God's grace according to the Christian teaching *(John 3: 16)*.

"I have come into the world, so that no one who believes in me should stay in darkness." (John 12:46).

CHAPTER THREE

Spiritual and Physical Balanced Diet

The Bible which is God's word to us says, *"God is love."* *1 John 4:7-8*. This universal living and immortal God loves all the people in the world and He provides them with spiritual and physical food for their existence on earth. He urges them to take the responsibility given to them and if they neglect their responsibility to eat for their existence, they become irresponsible stewards of themselves and others which is a sign that they do not love themselves. The second greatest commandment in the Bible is *"Love your neighbour as yourself." Matthew 22:39*. If you love yourself, you do not harm yourself physically and spiritually according to the holistic understanding of a person. The good things we do to ourselves, we should do to others as expected of us to do by God our Maker and Owner for our mutual good physically and spiritually. Refusal to follow God's instructions for our salvation leads to sin and eternal death if we do not repent for God to forgive us.

God, the Provider of all things we have, expects us all to give services to those in need of them. Out of love and kindness, we choose to be other people's servants. Other people's service for welfare gives joy to the givers of necessary services to the glory of God our Owner and Saviour. Scientists have discovered that nutrients in balanced diets are of necessity for the body to be healthy. Lack of this balanced diet causes some physical deficiencies that can only be corrected by the right nutrients needed by the body. The food we eat is medicine for the body and failure to take it, has serious consequences like malfunctioning of body systems and even loss of life.

When we prepare different types of food and satisfy our hunger though this can be difficult and monotonous, it is worth doing for our existence. The same applies to spiritual matters. The inner person which is the soul is the complementary part of the body that makes a person. It needs the food that is abstract as the soul itself is also abstract. The food for spiritual and moral growth is the transforming and enriching word of God besides secular social teachings that might be right or wrong and misleading in the upbringing of a person mentally and spiritually. If good teachings from the Bible, philosophy and science positively influence the inner person to see things well, the whole person acts responsibly. This is like the taking of balanced diet by the body whose food is concrete, actual or tangible, all of which are needed by it to function well. However, Christian theological teachings, all of which are based on the Bible, are commendable in leading the believers to God for their salvation from sin.

Reading the Bible to understand, singing hymns in order to share spiritual experiences with the composers, fathers and mothers of our church, preaching the Word of God, praying ceaselessly and teaching the word of God, strengthens a Christian culture or tradition in order to be connected to God, the source of life and the power to conquer the tempter in life.

All these religious phenomena practised in worship constitute living a life of worship in the society which can help to transform people to live as the disciples and apostles of Jesus spiritually and morally. Singing hymns inspires the worshippers and encourages them to trust in God under all life situations. The writer has been helped in the faith journey by some of the hymns like: "O God our help in ages past" and "The Lord is my shepherd." The testimonies of the composers make the old and new members dauntless in their ministries as they serve God and the people. Reading the words of the hymns and singing them with understanding makes the participants in worship realise that God helped the believers in the past as He does His church today to prove His immutability. Let us reflect on the following hymns:

O God Our Help in Ages Past

O God, our Help in ages past,
Our hope for years to come,
Our shelter from the stormy blast,
And our eternal home.

Under the shadow of Thy throne,
Thy Saints have dwelt secure;
Sufficient is thine arm alone,
And our defence is sure.

Before the hills in order stood,
or earth received its frame,
From everlasting Thou art God,
To endless years the same.

A thousand ages in Thy sight,
Are like an evening gone,
Short as the watch that ends the night,
Before the rising sun.

Time like an ever-rolling stream,
Bears all its sons away;
They fly forgotten, as a dream
Dies at the opening day.

O God, our help in ages past.
Our hope for years to come;
Be Thou our guard while life
Shall last,
And our eternal home.

The Lord is my Shepherd

The Lord's my shepherd, I'll not want;
He makes me down to lie
In pastures green; He leadeth me
The quiet waters by.

My soul He doth restore again, And me to walk doth, make
Within the paths of righteousness,
E'en for His own name's sake

Yea, though I walk in death's dark vale,
Yet will I fear no ill;
For Thou Art with, and Thy rod
And staff me comfort still

My table Thou hast furnished.
In presence of my foes;
My head Thou dost with oil anoint,
And my cup overflows

Goodness and mercy my life
Shall surely follow me,
And in God's house forevermore
My dwelling-place shall be.

Tell Me Old, Old Story

Tell me the old, old story
Of unseen things above,
Of Jesus and, His glory,
Of Jesus and His love.
Tell me the story simply,
As for I am weak and weary,
And helpless and defiled.

Refrain

Tell me the old, old story;
Tell me the old, old story,
Tell me the old, old story
Of Jesus and His love

Tell me the story slowly,
That I may take it in-
That wonderful redemption,
God's remedy for sin.
Tell me the story often,
For I forget so soon;
The early dew of morning
Has passed away at noon [*Refrain*]

Tell me the same old story,
When you have cause to fear,
That this world's empty glory,
Is costing me too dear.
Tell me the story always,
If you would really be,
In any time of trouble,
A comforter to me [*Refrain*]

Author: Kate Hankey

Worshipping While Adhering to Faith and Hope

Valuable lessons can be learnt about living the life of worship from the Jewish young men among others who were called the chosen ones of God, upholding unwavering faith in God alone. These young men were Daniel, Hananiah, Mishael and Azariah who were given new Babylonian names, Belteshazzar, Shadrack, Misheck and Abednego respectively under the Babylonian captivity. Daniel and his three friends mentioned with him earlier on, had profound belief in one true God, the Creator of heaven and earth and they did not want to be defiled by eating the royal food and wine. Daniel asked that he and his friends be given vegetables only to eat and water to drink for ten days during their preparation for suitability selection to serve the king's palace. They were to be taught the language and literature of the Babylonians. The king assigned them a daily amount of food and wine from the king's table. They were to be trained for three years and after that, they were to enter the king's service. After ten days preparation to be tested for suitability to serve in the king's palace, the four Jewish candidates were found to be healthier and better nourished than any of the Babylonian candidates who ate the royal food. God was with the four Jewish, humble men who chose to obey Him by refusing to drink wine. This means that they were self-disciplined or they were clever enough to apply the virtuous ethical principle of self-control. It is wise to choose what to eat from what not to eat or to be sober in judgement in order to avoid living dangerously in life. The Bible says, *"The fear of the Lord is the beginning of wisdom, and knowledge of the Holy One is understanding." Proverbs 9:10.*

These four Jewish friends and fearers of God excelled in the subjects they were studying. At the end of their period of study, they were brought to King Nebuchadnezzar. The King talked to them and found that none of the young men with whom they had been chosen for suitability test to serve in the king's palace matched them in wisdom and understanding. The four

Jewish men were ten times better than all the magicians and enchanters in the king's whole kingdom. When God chooses or calls you and you humble yourself before Him, He equips you with wisdom and understanding to operate well and effectively in the society to the glory of God Himself who should be worshipped.

The hidden thing about obeying or faith in God is His transcendence which Jesus, His only begotten Son revealed to mankind in His teachings in parables and simple explanations about God the Father, His kingdom, citizens of God's kingdom, how to enter the kingdom of God while still on earth and the consummation of God's kingdom in eternity. Such teachings are considered mythical, meaningless, incomprehensible and only suitable to be relegated by some people who consider themselves wiser according to secular standards devoid of faith. It is faith, the gift of God to us *(Ephesians 2:8-9)* which when sincerely accepted helps to open the doors to the obscure wealth of reality by God's grace. According to the letter of Hebrews, there is a spiritual eye-opener for us in relation to the significance of faith as a gift extended to all the people which can be accepted or not depending on our decision. Faith is not to be forced on people but to be voluntarily accepted by the hearers of the word of God through reasoning and guidance of the Holy Spirit. The writer of the letter of Hebrews says: *"Therefore, since we are surrounded by such a great cloud of witnesses, let us throw off everything that hinders and the sin that so easily entangles. And let us run with perseverance the race marked out for us, fixing our eyes on Jesus, the pioneer and perfector of faith, for the joy set before him he endured the cross, scorning its shame, and sat down at the right hand of the throne. Consider him who endured such opposition from sinners, so that you will not grow weary and lose heart."* Hebrews 12:1-3.

The four Jewish friends obeyed God and refrained from taking the forbidden food according to their dietary laws and the Lord drew closer to them in order to give them wisdom and knowledge. In living the worship life, there are permissible things to be done because they are aligned to the will of God and forbidden things because they are against the will of God. Drunkenness impairs reasoning and can lead the drunkard to behave irresponsibly, publicly to their disgrace and even to the disgrace of the onlookers. Those who obey God are supposed to guide others to be people of integrity by using the wisdom given to them by God. Self-control that results from obeying God or faith in God is one of the fruits of the Holy Spirit as expressed in his letter to the *Galatians 5:23*. To behave responsibly in the world with so many temptations that can mislead people to divert from what they ought to be in light of God, the Holy One. People who may be weak and vulnerable in the service of the Lord in face of many social problems are spiritually strengthened to do great things by God who works secretly, convincingly and powerfully in them to effect the purpose for them to achieve for their good and the glory of God Himself.

The significance of obedience to God has been expressed so well in the book of Daniel through the devoted worshippers of God - Shadrach, Misheck and Abednego who were thrown into the blazing furnace of fire heated seven times for their insubordination to the king's orders to worship an idol. The decalogue or ten commandments states - only the Holy living and immortal God is to be worshipped. The three young believers appeared conspicuously to be following their Jewish laws and strict worship of one true God. For their refusal to worship an idol, they were thrown into the blazing furnace but much to the surprise of the king and his fellow onlookers, they saw a fourth man who looked like a Son of God among the three Jewish men who had been thrown into the furnace. This is a true visible indication of God's intervention in the persecution of innocent people to save them for His plan to be achieved. What God plans to do cannot be stopped by anyone even if His messengers can be humiliated or put to death because of their faith in God. People can destroy the body but they cannot destroy soul. It is only God who can destroy both body and soul in hell as what Jesus said in *Mattew 1:28*.

Social malpractices are avoidable if social norms and values based Theocentric or Christocentric ethical values like: Agape love which is unconditional, kindness, self-control, faithfulness, forgiveness, diligence, respect, trustworthiness, empathy, endurance, patience and selflessness are followed. Such moral virtues are to be aimed at in daily living. Interdependence should be regarded as the normal way or norm for human co-existence instituted by God our owner and the Sovereign Ruler of the universe. Bad attitudes result in bad behaviour which turns human situations to resemble animalistic situations governed by the of the survival of the fittest or the law of the jungle.

Christians are expected to aim high in the spirituality and morality as they adhere to the life of worship in order to please God and to be connected to Him. Christian servitude to the Creator entails loving God and the people and sacrifice in transforming the world to be a better place to live in for love, justice, righteousness, peace, development and prosperity will certainly prevail.

God calls all people to have an intimate relationship with Him but he does not force them to enter into His fellowship with Him. To be a Christian or not depends on one's decision through one's reasoning. However, the choice to obey or disobey God has repercussions which are rewardable or condemnable in the life to come after this life on earth *(Romans 14:10; 2 Corinthians 5:10; Ecclesiastes 12:14)*.

Daniel, a Jewish Babylonian captive who practised worship life was also persecuted by being thrown into the lion's den to be eaten up because of his faith in God. A miracle happened; the hungry lions just looked at a person who was supposed to be prey as inedible. This event surprised the king and the spectators to the extent of the king calling out to Daniel early in the morning the following day to say, "Daniel, the servant of the living God, has your God, whom you serve continually, been able to rescue you from the lions?" *Daniel 6:20*. In response to the king, Daniel said, *"May the live forever! My God sent his angel, and he shut the mouths of the lions. They have not hurt me, because I was found innocent in his sight. Nor have I ever done any wrong before you, your majesty." Daniel 6:22*. The king was happy and gave orders to lift Daniel out of the den. Those who falsely accused Daniel and their families were thrown into the den where they were overpowered and crushed. King Darius acknowledged the mighty God of the Jews and wrote to his people thus: *"I issue a decree that in every part of my kingdom people must fear and revere the God of Daniel. For he is the Living God and he endures forever. His kingdom will not be destroyed, his dominion will never end. He rescues and he saves; he performs signs and wonders in the heavens and on the earth. He has rescued Daniel from the power of the lions." Daniel 6:25-27*. The truth about God was said by king Darius an unbeliever to his subjects in order to accept the true God worshipped by the Jews in captivity. It is God who takes the initiative to reveal Himself in various ways for the people to know Him by reasoning in order to be converted. Even today, some people believe in God after having seen miraculous things he does which are beyond human comprehension and practicality.

To live the life of worship is to have God, people and self in mind. Doing the will of God is to live righteously and justly in the world and peace prevails for good standards of living spiritually, socially, politically, economically. Disobeying God results in many adverse social issues that make people restless, feeble and miserable owing to unreasonable violation of God-given human rights. People were not created to suffer and live miserably in the world but to live happily in communion with God and gratefully to Him for His care providence to people who are expected to be responsible stewards of the created things on earth. Is this kind of living possible or just imaginary?

With the help of God, what is viewed impossible is possible if we incline our ears to the divine counsel spiritually and morally. Jesus taught about the impossibility becoming the possibility through faith and by God's grace. On our own we can do what we are able to do. What is beyond our capability is beyond our reach. What God permits to happen, happens contrary to our world views or expectations to our great amazement. Jesus' and the apostles' miracles in the Bible are beyond common and scientific or philosophical knowledge because they are supernatural divine activities.

Miracles are possible and real even in our time because they happen through the power of God not that of a person. In faith healing, it is God who heals people through the person He chooses to do the healing momentarily for as long as He wants them to play the role. Healing through prayers is possible according to God's power and permission. The church has been given various gifts of the Spirit to use as required in and outside the church in Jesus' name *(1 Corinthians 12:1-11)*.

There is power in the blood of Jesus and in prayer which Jesus used in public and private places to be in communion with God the Father. Such a prayerful practice is what we ought to adopt in living the worship life for our and other people's benefit. Drawing near to God makes God draw near to us for guidance and protection and motivation *(James 4:8; Psalm 73:28; Isaiah 1:18; Matthew 11:28-30)*. To draw near to God is to trust Him and develop a deep, personal relationship with Him through worship that includes prayers, fasting, singing and deeds. By so doing, we aim at living a righteous life which is required of us by God our Creator.

Jesus' Moments of Worship

Jesus prayed to His Father in heaven though He was God the Son. This shows the need for us to resort to prayer in different life situations to be in communion with God who sees, hears and responds to our prayers. Jesus prayed during His baptism *(Luke 3:21-22)*, in demanding moments *(Matthew 4:1-13; Mark 1:9-13; Luke 4:14-30)*; in decision-making to choose His disciples *(Luke 6:12)*; during special time with God the Father *(Luke 5:16)*; when he was transfigured in the company of Peter, John and James *(Luke 9:28)*; in Gethsemane while in of God the Father's support *(Luke 22:40-44* and while in great pain on the cross *(Luke 23:34; Matthew 27:46)*; praying for His disciples *(John 17:9)* and Jesus praying for all believers *(John 17:20-26)*. Jesus lived the life of worship to be in communion with God the Father and God the Holy Spirit. In support of Jesus' custom of praying to be in communion with God the Father, Paul wrote in His letter to *1 Thessalonians 5:16-22, "Rejoice always, pray continually, give thanks in all circumstances; for this is God's will for you in Christ Jesus. Do not quench the Spirit. Do not treat prophecies with contempt but test them all, hold on to what is good, reject every kind of evil."*

In Gethsemane Jesus alerted His disciples to be vigilant as they live in the world to avert temptations that mislead the people in their spirit of worship. In *Matthew 26:41* Jesus said, *"Watch and pray so that you will not fall into temptation."* The Spirit is willing, but the flesh is weak. The tempter strikes strongly and easily when we feel weak to be vigilant and prayerful. This is the opportune time for the devil to attack whoever is not alert. The tempter tactfully stalks the carefree people to victimise them. When we wander away from the Saviour we can be snatched away by the devil and be fed spiritual deadly food whose results are also poisonous to those who get it from us. Human beings are spiritually, physically and morally vulnerable without God's assistance that comes to us through obedience all the time.

Life without the past is like a tree whose roots have been cut. It is bound to perish miserably. Learning from other people who lived before us will enrich our present life by avoiding the mistakes they made but taking in what they did well in life.

Norms and values are derived from the past to be followed in the present if still relevant to time and conditions compatible with the teachings of God. New world views, despite their newness, are not to be acceptable if they contradict the will of God. Anything that severs the relationship of God with human beings is to be avoided to be connected to God in attitudes and deeds.

The gospel writers and the apostles of Jesus inspired by the Holy Spirit wrote about normative and virtuous principles to guide the Christian believers as born-again people spiritually and coheirs of Jesus Christ. Christian life is not to be talked about only but it is to be lived. It helps in the transformation of attitudes, behaviour and culture for a better spiritual and moral living in any social culture. Although not all can adopt the Christian teachings for various reasons, Jesus in His Great Commission ordered His followers who were later known as the Christians or the church to go into the whole world to teach the people and preach to them about the new faith in God through Himself and lay emphasis on repentance from sin in order to be baptised in the name of the Triune God for their salvation from sin and eternal death hereafter *(John 3:1-16)*. Jesus urges people to follow Him in order to move freely in the faith journey to eternal life hence He said to His disciples *(John 8:31-38; Matthew 28:16-20; Luke 9:23-24; John 13:34-35; John 15:16-17; Matthew 11:28-30 and John 14:6.* Jesus said, *"I am the way and the truth and the life. No one comes to the Father except through me."* The Christians' belief in ultimate salvation from sin and the second eternal death to come is based on Jesus Christ the Lamb of God, *"Agnus Dei"* (*Latin*) who died on the cross for the sins of mankind. Such teachings make up the Christian Doctrine of Soteriology *(John 3:16)*. Jesus our only hope of salvation for we all fall short of God's glory. Paul says in *Romans 3:21-24, "But now apart from the Law the righteousness of God has been made known, to which the Law and the Prophets testify. This righteousness is given through faith in Jesus to all who believe. There is no difference between Jew and Gentile for all have sinned and fall short of the glory of God, and all are justified freely by his grace through the redemption that came by Jesus Christ."* God presented Christ as a sacrifice of atonement, through the shedding of his blood - to be received by faith. He did this to demonstrate his righteousness because in his forbearance he had left the sins committed beforehand unpunished - he did it to demonstrate his righteousness at the present time, so as to be just and one who justifies those who have faith in Jesus. *(Romans 3:21-26).* What God has done for us in His Son Jesus is affirmed in the hymn that follows:

What Can Wash Away My Sin
Nothing But the Blood

1. What can wash away my sin
Nothing but the blood of Jesus
What can make me whole again
Nothing but the blood of Jesus
Oh precious id the flow, that makes
Me white as snow
No other fount I know
Nothing but the blood of Jesus

2. For my pardon, yes I see
Nothing but the blood of Jesus
For my cleansing there's my plead
Nothing but the blood of Jesus
Oh precious is the flow that makes
Me white as snow
No other fount I know
Nothing but the blood of Jesus

3. Nothing can for sin atone
Nothing but the blood of Jesus
Not of good that I have done
Nothing but the blood of Jesus
Oh precious is the flow that makes
Me white as snow
No other fount I know
Nothing but the blood of Jesus

4. This is all my hope and peace
Nothing but the blood of Jesus
This is all my righteous mess
Nothing but the blood of Jesus
Oh precious is the flow that makes
Me white as snow
No other fount I know
Nothing but the blood of Jesus

Obeying what God the Father and God the Son is getting into the right high way to eternal home of the saved ones from sin, knowing the truth that liberates from sin which is a hindrance to communication with God. Unpardoned sin is deadly whereas true repentance from sin and God's forgiveness lead to eternal life through faith in Jesus and by God's grace *(John 3:16)*.

CHAPTER FOUR

True Worship in Life

True worship in life for the living God the Creator of Heaven and earth is based on the two greatest commandments which are: Loving God and loving fellow people as we love ourselves *(Matthew 22:34-37)*.

The worship of God is to be done seven days in a week. The number seven indicates completeness. Worship should not only be going to church on a Sunday only or during church calendared events like Christmas Day, Holy Week or Passion Week. Some Christians appear in the sanctuary on the day of Baptism of their children confirmation of adults into full membership, the Eucharist, wedding, revival gathering and for funeral services. Fellowship of believers as the body of Jesus should be encouraged to be carried out at the opportune time as need demands individually, in groups or corporately in order to commune with the Creator the source of wisdom, comfort and inspiration to do His will under all circumstances. By coming together from time to time to worship helps the worshippers to inspire one another as they experience the presence of God through listening to the word of God, singing hymns, songs and choruses of praising the Lord. Teachings and preaching of the word of God nourish the soul and strengthens it spiritually in the life journey against spiritual adverse and harmful circumstances. Corporate inclusive worship is appropriate for those who hunger and thirst after righteousness for God only can satisfy them miraculously. There is exclusive worship which is made up of a group of people mentally agreeing to meet for their agreed upon purpose at their convenient time! Of necessity also is the personal and private worship to deepen one's faith in God by reflecting on the word of God, praying and singing hymns like, "Take time to be holy."

> Take time to be holy, speak often with the Lord;
> Abide in Him always, and feed on His word.
> Make friends of God's children, help those who are weak,
> Forgetting in nothing His blessing to seek
>
> Take time to be holy, the world rushes on;
> Spend much time in secret, with Jesus alone
> By looking to Jesus, like Him thou shalt be;
> Thy friends in thy conduct His likeness shall see
>
> Take time to be holy, let Him be thy guide;
> And run not before Him, whatever be tide
> In joy or in sorrow, still follow the Lord,
> And, looking to Jesus, still trust in His word
>
> Take time to be holy, be calm in thy soul,
> Each thought and each motive beneath His control
> Thus led by His Spirit to fountains of love,
> Thou soon shalt be fitted for service above.

In 'Chronos' time (ordinary time in which we carry out our daily duties), we should have 'Kyros' time which is a very special time for intimate relationship with God to talk to Him and hear from Him to get inspiration, guidance, protection and strength in doing His work in the world which is the Lord's vineyard. Conversion of the people and repentance are very important religions phenomena that lead to salvation now and ultimately hereafter, to inherit eternal life through faith in Jesus and by God's grace *(John 3:16).*

Christians as Disciples and Apostles of Jesus

When Jesus was preaching on the mountain, He metaphorically referred to His followers as the salt and the light of the earth *(Matthew 5:13-16)*, meaning they were given the responsibility to preserve the norms and values to be observed and to impart to others for their spiritual and moral guidance to please God. They were to play the role of healing and protecting the souls of the people from being corrupted by sin! Salt during that time was used to preserve meat from rotting and for making relish palatable just as the word of God makes the believers acceptable before God, their Maker through their faith and deeds. Salt was also used in washing wounds when healing the wounded people just as faith in God, good attitudes and behaviour are therapeutic to the sick and the wounded physically and spiritually in pastoral care of the people. Faith healing is possible in the Christian faith. What a suitable metaphor for Christians salt is! When this salt keeps its essence, it plays its role effectively as it is meant to do but when it loses its saltness, it becomes useless and only fit to be thrown away. The followers or disciples of Jesus who learn from Jesus are supposed to be faithful and dependable in carrying out their responsibilities according to their calling to be effective in transforming the world to be a better habitable place by maintaining the theological norms and values as spiritual and moral principles that can guide attitudes and behaviour for the welfare, safety and salvation of the people from sin. People are supposed to be their brothers' and sisters' keepers as they strive to live peacefully and harmoniously under the Rule of God by whom and for when they were created in His image 'imago Dei' - image of God.

Jesus also referred to His followers or disciples who were His learners, as the light of the world meaning that they should guide those who needed spiritual and moral assistance to be faithful disciples of Jesus who is the way to the Father, the truth that liberates from ignorance of the Triune God and the sins that lead to death and the one who is capable of giving life through faith in Him. Jesus is the only hope for our salvation from sin *(John 14:6)*. Jesus is coeternal with God the Father and God the Holy Spirit as the three persons in their Trinity. This is the nature of the living and immortal God. The Christians' belief in God through faith in Jesus as they strive to live a righteous life according to the word of God in the Bible transforms them spiritually and morally and makes them fit to be the light of the world infested with many temptations or snares that mislead and catch those who are not vigilant in the life journey. The disciples of Jesus should be good stewards of their lives as they should be good stewards of other people's lives in the world. By teaching about God and His kingdom on earth and hereafter, through attitudes and behaviour they can shine to show others the way to salvation as meant to be done by the Lord, to live like this is to live the life of worship in the society. The mission of God *'Missio Dei'* (*Latin*) in the world for our salvation and the mission of the church 'Missio Ecclesia' work hand in glove for the salvation of mankind from sin through faith in Jesus Christ and by God's grace. Christian theology expresses the truth about the Christian faith in a consistent and coherent manner which helps people to reason in making the decision to declare more reasonably than not to follow Jesus. Christians should be humble servants - not leaders in religious matters, who seek self-popularity, at the expense of raising the banner of Jesus who should be worshipped for what He is and what He does through us as demonstrated by Peter and John the disciples and apostles of Jesus in *Acts 3:11-16*. Peter wanted the onlookers to praise Jesus but not Peter himself and John for the healing of a lame man at the temple gate of Beautiful. A miracle of healing is a manifestation of the presence of God who should be acknowledged and worshipped sincerely.

The restoration of people who have decided to be liberated from doing what pleases them though contrary to the will of God, is part of the mission of God in the world. Jesus' vicarious suffering and death as His mission on earth, were for our sake to be redeemed from sin. The mission of the church as the body of Christ continues this process of salvation through preaching and teaching the word of God effectively in the world for people to be saved by God Himself. Let's always feed on the word of God, by accepting it as thee spiritual food given to the people by Jesus as He said in *John 6:35, "I am the bread of life. Whoever comes to me will never go hungry, and whoever believes in me will never be thirsty."* Jesus gives the living water, the spiritual sustenance of salvation when we accept Him as our personal Saviour. Jesus also said, *"but whoever drinks the water I give them will never thirst. Indeed, the water I give them will become in them a spring of water welling up to eternal life." (John 4:14).* In *John 7:37-38*, Jesus said, *"Let anyone who is thirsty come to me and drink. Whoever believes in me as scripture has said, rivers of the living water will flow from within them."* The compassionate caring Lord Jesus once said, *"Come to me, all you who are weary and burdened, and I will give you rest. Take my yoke upon you and learn from me, for I am gentle and humble in heart, and you will find rest for your souls. For my yoke is easy and my burden is light." (Matthew 11:28-30)* The yoke is obedience or faith and his burden is the faith that should be carried always, whose spiritual weight is lighter to bear than the burden of sin that keeps on haunting you when you are awake or asleep in dreams. Because of what Jesus put into practice and what He taught the people during His mission of God, the Christians experience the passion to live the life of worship as individuals privately, exclusive groups and corporate congregations in the church or religious revivals. In these places and situations, believers would like to have an encounter with the Lord and Saviour in a special and organised way to interact with the Lord by singing songs of thanksgiving, exalting Him, sending their petitions, interceding for other people and life situations.

Encounter with the Lord enriches the soul, gives insights, courage comfort, guidance, feeling of forgiveness and hope for a brighter future on earth and in life to come in heaven, basing on what is said in *John 3:16* in the Bible. To live responsibly is to care for your whole self-body, mind and soul as you should also care for others to be in good state required of them by the Lord for us all. These beliefs and practices encourage the believers to cling to their faith in hope of seeing what they cannot see but, yet to be seen by the saved ones hereafter. Living the worship life, reminds the writer of two spiritually motivating hymns that urge worshippers to continue to do the practices that draw them to the Lord as they aspire to live a righteous life on earth with the help of God. These hymns are the following:

Sweet Hour of Prayer

Sweet hour of prayer! Sweet hour of hour of prayer!
That calls me from a world of care,
And bids me at my Father's throne
Make all my wants and wishes known.
In seasons of distress and grief,
My soul has often found relief.
And oft escaped the tempter's snare,
By thy return, sweet hour of prayer!

Sweet hour or prayer! Sweet hour of prayer!
The joys I feel, the bliss I share,
Of those whose anxious spirits burn
With strong desires for thy return!
With such I hasten to the place
Where God my Saviour shows His face,
And gladly take my station there,
And wait for thee for thee, sweet hour of prayer!

Sweet hour or prayer! Sweet hour or prayer!
Thy wings shall my petition bear
To Him whose truth and faithfulness

Engage the waiting soul to bless.
And since He bids me seek His face,
Believe His word and trust His grace,
I'll cast on Him my every care,
And wait for thee, sweet hour of prayer!

Sweet hour of prayer! Sweet hour of prayer!
May I thy consolation share,
Till, from Mount Pisgah lofty height,
I view my home and take my flight.
This robe of flesh I'll drop, and rise
To seize the everlasting prize,
And shout while passing through the air,
"Farewell, farewell, sweet hour of prayer!"

Source: Faith Publishing House Evening Light songs, 1949, edited 1987 (312).

Like the hymn "Sweet Hour of Prayer," is the hymn, "I come to the Garden Alone," draws the worshipper closer to God. While alone during the 'kyros' time encounter with the Lord, to enable you to pour your heart to him for He sees, hears and responds according to His time. Remember, Jesus Christ's experience in Gethsemane where the enemies thought they had defeated Jesus by arresting Him but the Easter Sunday came and proved them wrong when the Lord Jesus resurrected from the dead, to fulfil the salvation plan of God that the redemption of mankind from sin would be through His Son's death on the cross. Here is another hymn that has a spiritual impact on a worshipper in solitude:

I come to the Garden Alone

I come to the Garden alone,
While the due is still on the roses;
And the voice I hear, falling on my ear,
The Son of God discloses.

Refrain

And He walks with me, and He talks with me,
And He tells me I am His own,
And the joy we share as we tarry there,
None other has ever known.

He speaks, and the sound of His voice
Is so sweet the birds hush their singing;
And the melody that He gave to me
Within my heart is ringing. [*Refrain*]

I'd stay in the garden with Him
Tho' the night around me be failing;
But He bids me go; thro' the voice of woe,
His voice to me is calling. [*Refrain*]

Baptism Hymnal, 1991. Author: C. Austin Miles.

Prayerful life is enjoyed in living the worship life. Those who have established this type of living concur that there are different types of prayers for different situations as worshippers interact with God and these are: Prayers of worship and adoration where God is given His glory worthiness because of what or who He is as our Owner and Saviour. There is no one like Him in heaven, on earth omnipresent, omniscient and immortal. God is the source of wisdom which He shares graciously to all the people He created in His image to serve Him and fellow people to His joy and glory.

There are prayers of thanksgiving in light of God's providence. These prayers are said to God to show our gratitude to God for what He did in creation, in human history. What He does to us in different life situations and what we hope He will finally do to the saved ones through their faith and by His grace *(John 3:16)*. When we go and to bed and wake up in the morning, we should know that sleeping is not just a natural phenomenon which functions without God's control. Night comes for us to rest and morning comes for us to go out and serve God, fellow people and ourselves for sustenance. It is God who enables us to sleep at night and rise in the morning. Consequently, we need to give a thanksgiving prayer to the Almighty. God is in control of all life situations hence He is omnipotent. Our lives are in His hands hence we should say thanksgiving prayers to Him whose unmerited grace keeps life going to its stipulated end on earth. God provides us with air, rains, sunshine, food, strength to do work, health, children and other things we need for our existence without which, we cannot live.

Socially, grateful children please their parents by being thankful for what their parents do to them for their welfare, protection and guidance in life. Because God loves us beyond our expectations despite our sinfulness or disobedience, He loves us and gives us time to repent wholeheartedly to be forgiven here on earth so as to have our sins forgiven and have eternal life after our resurrection from the dead, we ought to be grateful to Him! God loves us and we should love Him too by worshipping Him for what He is and what He does to Him. To obey what He says, is to honour, love Him and is to acknowledge Him to be our Father in heaven who is also everywhere. When we praise God we reciprocate His love through prayers of thanksgiving and promoting benevolence through charity activities to the needy in order to raise high the people's standard of living by giving support spiritually, morally and materially. Living the life of worship will surely transform the people's standard of living. There are prayers said to God seeking direction and guidance in decision-making doing things with clear conscience and rightfully in light of God and to the joy of people who God loves indiscriminately although He hates the sins they commit which they should repent to avoid His anger which at the end of life will result in eternal death. In His sermon on the mount, He taught, His listeners how to communicate with God in *Matthew 7:7-8:* *"Ask and it will be given to you; seek you will find; knock and the door will be opened to you. For everyone who asks receives; the one who seeks finds; and to the one who knocks the door will be opened."*

What the Lord teaches is to be put into practice for that is what a faithful disciple of Jesus is supposed to do to be effective in the mission of the church - *"Missio Ecclesia."* Jesus told a parable of the importunate or persistent widow in *Luke 18:1-8*, to show the importance of praying ceaselessly and God, at His own time, will respond to the prayer. Any answer given to our request, is done in His righteousness. God knows what is good for us and why what we ask for is not granted or deferred to a later time. In some cases, we would like to have an urgent response to our requests and become disappointed when things happen contrary to our expectations. There are times when we ask with ulterior negative motives to harm ourselves or others when we ask for wealth, power, promotion and other possessions to be used selfishly at other people's disadvantages. Maybe, we are better off spiritually and morally without some of the things we would like to have. Life is not only those we want to have but much more than those. Most of the things that we need in life already been provided to us like: life, air, water, food, health, education, wisdom, employment, faith, shelter, clothes, means of transport, children, husbands and wives. You may have worked hard to have some of them but theologically speaking those are given to us graciously by God for our welfare. At times we might not have all of them but might have the necessary things to live. Some of the things we ask for are for luxury but life can go on comfortably without them. Some of the things we ask may be truly, assets that can end as liabilities if they are managed unskilfully. There are times when people are blessed with wealth but end up being paupers, demoralised and faithless. In all life situations, those who live the life of worship should cling to their faith in God who is the provider of the things we have. Even certain things may be beyond our reach although we try hard to reach them, this should not weaken us spiritually or morally to the extent of falling into apostasy but endure to live in hope of a brighter future here on earth through righteous means with the ultimate goal - the eternal life in heaven. We should faithfully endeavour to work diligently, to acquire wealth if possible and use it to benefit us and other people who might need our help for the less fortunate will always be in the world. The words said by the Prophet Habakkuk in his prayer, should be borne in mind and be our attitude when those things we want to have are unavailable. Here is the helpful advice to all believers in God: though the fig tree does not bud and there are no grapes on the vines, though the olive crop fails and the fields produce no food, though there are no sheep in the pen and no cattle in the stalls, yet I will rejoice in the Lord, I will be joyful in God my Saviour *(Habakkuk 3:17-18)*.

Wise people have become what they are today by learning from God others who lived before them and their contemporaries. Let us always be learners to be good decision-makers and doers of the things that can be emulated by others in the society we happen to find ourselves like what our Lord Jesus said in *Matthew 5:16, "In the same way, let your light shine before others, that they may see your good deeds and glorify your Father in heaven."* Let's aim at leaving a good and long-lasting legacy that will impact and benefit others in the society for ages.

As in the past, faith healing is possible today by using the gift of the Holy Spirit as stated in the Bible. It is God who heals through the believers chosen by Him to do the work *(1 Corinthians 12:4-11)*. However, most of the Christians can be healed in the hospitals also because God can use any method of healing as He chooses it is God who heals through people. Herbalists can heal some of the ailments using medicinal plants but some people hesitate to be treated by them because their medicines are not scientifically measured and they might cause uncontrollable side effects. Most believers avoid to be treated by traditional magical healers because of their beliefs in the powers of the ancestral living dead lest they might fall into idolatry or dualism. As trinitarian monotheists, Christians avoid approaching the magical healers because of their scientifically untrained status and their religious background that are contradictory to the Christian faith as they may have immeasurable extracts from the scientifically approved medicinal plants. Because of social situations that affect people in the society like ailments, social sins, unemployment, hunger, hopelessness, deaths and loss of belongings which cause the state of bereavement, people need some prayers to comfort them as they travel the life journey. Without spiritual and moral support through prayers and material support, some become destitute. There may be others who cannot withstand the problems and get into suicidal tendencies. When they are given spiritual, moral and material support through some counselling, they might become resilient and fight for their living much to their surprise. The intercessors pray for God's intervention as they believe that the God they worship is the God of history and He is capable of changing bad situations for the better. Miracles like in the past can happen through prayers to God who is also known as El Roi (God who sees me) El Shaddai (God Almighty) El Olam (Everlasting God) Yahweh Rapha (The Lord who heals) to name a few names for the God whom the Christians worship. The faith that Christians hold can make it possible for miracles to take place through God's assistance. Some ailments can be cured whereas others can be incurable if God does not intervene leading to death which is interpreted according to the Christian belief that we cannot live beyond the limit of our life on earth that was set by God.

Death can strike unexpectedly among the young and adults according to the divine limit of set times to die as stated in *Ecclesiastes 3:1-2, "There is time for everything, and a season for every activity under the heavens: a time to be born and a time to uproot."* Prayers of intercession are very necessary for they are an expression of empathy or compassion to the suffering people which gives them hope for better peaceful situations through God's intervention for the restoration of order, peace and time of joy.

There are corporate prayers where worshippers gather together for spiritual communion with God as one body of our Lord Jesus to worship God. The participation of believers strengthen one another as they sing together thanking praising God. Testimonies given about God's activities among them encourage one another to cling to their faith under all circumstances. By so doing the worshippers grow spiritually and dedicate themselves to the Lord to serve Him and the people through evangelism sacrificially as they plan churches in new places. Living the life of worship is strongly backed by the Lord's prayer *(Matthew 6:9-13; Luke 11:1-4)*. In the Gospel according to St Luke, one of the disciples asked Jesus to teach them how to pray as John the Baptist taught his disciples how to pray. In response to the disciples' readiness to learn, Jesus as a teacher, knew that time had come to teach His disciples to teach a brief comprehensive prayer that would be the foundation of worship. Matthew emphasises the significance of saying short prayers that are said to the point without showing off for self-praise like what the unbelievers or pagans were doing. In *Matthew 6:7-8*, Jesus said thus: *"And when you pray, do not keep on babbling like pagans. For they think they will be heard because of their many words. Do not be like them, for your Father knows what you need before you ask him."* Having the right attitude and behaviour in worship like humbleness, reverence of God and orderliness, creates an atmosphere which is conducive to solemn worship to God who should be exalted with the reverence He deserves as the Lord and Saviour. In the Lord's Prayer, Jesus taught the disciples to start mentioning God as their Father. The Father of Jesus is the Father of the adopted children of God as they were born again through spiritual birth by believing in Jesus, as it is said in *John 1:12, "yet to all who did receive him, to those who believed in his name, he gave the right to become children of God-children born not of natural descent nor of human decision or a husband's will, but born of God."* The transcendent God is holy and dwells in heaven though omnipresent on earth, a characteristic which is uniquely divine. Worshippers should ask for the rule of God to be felt or experienced by people whom He created in His image (*Imago Dei*) on earth in order to have communion with God. Enjoying to have fellowship with God our Owner and Saviour, gives believers courage and profound faith to walk the spiritual journey whose results are good attitude and behaviour towards God and fellow people as we cohabit in the world, doing good of every kind indiscriminately among ourselves as what God does to us all. Living in the love that God loves us with, the agape love and peace brings about safety, development, unity and prosperity in the society. Such a situation makes people experience a state of blessedness as mentioned by Jesus in His sermon on the mount in *Matthew 5:3-12*, in His teaching on the beatitudes where the will of God is what ought to be done not our contradictory will which may be our desire that is abominable in the sight of God. Sin is the result of pride that is egocentric and denies what is right in the sight of God in order to satisfy one's selfish desires which may be physically, spiritually, and morally harmful to oneself and others. Such insubordination is disobedience which begets all sorts of sinful activities in any society. Paul having mentioned the acts of the flesh in *Galatians 5:19-21*, he went on to mention the fruit of the Spirit which should be manifested in children of God by saying: *"But the fruit of the Spirit is love, joy, peace, forbearance, kindness, goodness, faithfulness, gentleness and self-control. Against such things there is no law." (Galatians 5:22-23)*. Doing the will of God on earth as it is done in heaven is to live a righteous life on earth where people should prepare themselves spiritually and morally to be acceptable by God in eternity after the resurrection from the dead. Perfect peace is in heaven where there is no tempter to mislead the saved ones who will live in their perfection eternally. After acknowledging God the Holy One and His Kingdom that begins on earth through faith in Jesus, we send our petitions to our Father in heaven who sees, hears and responds at His appropriate time to His children's requests to meet their needs. Since God is the Provider of all things we ask Him to provide us with, He provides enough food for our welfare. Hunger is a condition that makes a person to be prone to temptation that can lead to sin just as when Jesus was tempted by the devil to turn stones to bread when He became hungry during His forty day period of fasting, as He was charting His way to save mankind through preaching, teaching, vicarious suffering and death on the cross as an expiation for people's sins rather than just providing food to the curious people who were eager to follow Jesus for the sake of filling their stomachs with food. In *John 6:25-27* some people were in search of Jesus mainly to be fed with the food physically and to witness the miracles that He was able to perform to satisfy their curiosity. They did not hunger after righteousness but they wanted to eat loaves of bread as they were fed earlier on by Jesus who said to them, *"very truly I tell you, you are looking for me, not because you saw the signs I performed but because you ate the loaves and had your fill. Do not work for food that spoils, but for food that endures to eternal life which the Son of Man will give you. For on him God the Father has placed his seal of approval."*

Jesus in His teachings, the need for believers to ask God to forgive them their sins as they forgive those who sin against them. The forgiveness of believers depends on whether they forgive those who sin against them. The worshippers of the living God should ask God not to allow them to get into temptations that visit them to move them away from following His will but deliver them from the devil who is bent on dissuading people to be rebellious against Him in thought, word and deed. God who is the universal Ruler, in His glory and power will reign over the people eternally. This Lord's prayer conscientises the children of God the Father whom they should revere and depend on for guidance, protection, perfect rule and salvation from sin in His Kingdom on earth and in heaven eternally.

Briefly, this is what living the worship life is, in the kingdom of God on earth which will be consummated in heaven where sin will be no more and the saved ones through faith in Jesus and by God's grace, will experience perfect peace and joy eternally under the rule of God. We were created for God first and foremost, to obey and worship Him as we endeavour to live a righteous or clean life on earth. We cannot be perfect on our own. It is through faith in Jesus Christ that we hope to enter heaven to live with God eternally when we are justified from sin by God's grace *(John 3:16)*. Time on earth, is time to prepare for eternal life hereafter, as we diligently work for our existence by God's grace. The safe place for human beings is near the Triune God who is our Lord and Saviour. To wander away from God is to live dangerously. The apostle Peter wrote in his first letter, *1 Peter 5:8-9*, warning the people on earth to be vigilant always so that the devil does not snatch us away from a safe place spiritually and morally. He said, *"Be alert and of sober mind. Your enemy the devil prowls around like a roaring lion looking for someone to devour. Resist him, standing firm in the faith, because you know that the family of believers throughout the world is undergoing the same kind of sufferings."* Jesus, in His sermon on the mount, encourages His believers to continue to do the work they were called for in order to transform the world. He said, *"In the same way, let your light shine before others, that they may see your good deeds and glorify your Father in heaven," (Matthew 5:16).*

Creating a conducive atmosphere of dialogue with the Lord is by worship where the presence of God is intimately experienced. Such an environment is like what Jesus implied in the Gospel according to John: *"Remain in me, as I also remain in you. No branch can bear fruit by itself; it must remain in the vine. Neither can you bear fruit unless you remain in me." (John 15:4)*. Jesus is everything we need for our salvation hence we believe and trust that He is the Saviour from sin. He helps us to live the life that pleases God. It is through faith in Jesus that enables us to become children of God and co-heirs with Jesus Christ *(John 1:12, Romans 8:17)*. Living the life of worship is to live the life of obedience, living as responsible citizens in thought, words and deeds. Under all circumstances, we should bear in mind that the living God is transcendent, almighty, invincible and in control of all situations, as the Sovereign Ruler of the entire universe who should be worshipped with reverence in words, singing and benevolent deeds towards people in need. The good and bad things we do to other people we do to God *(Matthew 25:31-46)*. The word of God is true and transformative in attitude and deeds to whoever takes it seriously to please the Creator by living a righteous life on earth.

One of the inspiring hymns that was composed by Charles Wesley called, "O for a Thousand Tongues to Sing," had this heading as an adoption from Charles Wesley's spiritual mentor, German born Moravian missionary Peter Böhler, who said, *"Had I a thousand tongues, I would praise God with them all."* The author of this book feels the same in praising God who chose him to be His image rather than a rock or plant. He was elevated to the highest status as an image of God Himself and a steward of all created things on earth. Through God's prevenient and justifying grace, he came to know God and acknowledged Him as his Creator, Owner, Saviour and the Sovereign Ruler of the universe. By His grace he lives and hopes to live eternally through faith in Jesus, His only begotten Son, the perfect revelation of God the Father to mankind and by God the Father's grace. By the author's reasoning and experiential theology, he finds no other way of salvation from sin and hope to be acceptable in heaven *(John 3:16)*. Read or sing the words of Charles Wesley's hymn:

O For a Thousand Tongues to Sing

O for a thousand tongues to sing,
My great Redeemer's praise,
The glories of my God and King,
The triumphs of His grace.

My gracious Master and my God,
Assist me to proclaim,
To spread through all the earth abroad,
The honours of thy name.

Jesus! The name that charms our fears,
That bids our sorrows cease;
'Tis music in the sinner's ears,
'Tis life, and health, and peace

His love my heart has captive made,
His captive would I be
For He was bound, and scourged and died,
My captive soul to free

He breaks the power of cancelled sin,
He sets the prisoner free;
His blood can make the foulest clean;
His blood availed for me.

So now Thy blessed Name I love,
Thy will would e'er be mine
Had I a thousand hearts to give,
My Lord, they all were Thine!

In this hymn, Charles Wesley joyously sings God's forgiving love and its power to transform lives to be acceptable in the sight of God. Oh, what an inspiring hymn that gives hope to the hopeless because of our sinfulness!

CHAPTER FIVE

The People's Divine Experiences of the Triune God

God the Father

God the Father, the Creator of the heaven and earth, is the only true living and immortal God to be worshipped because of what He is and what He does to the created things according to His divine plan in His holiness. Our God is the God of history known as the Alpha and Omega as stated in *Isaiah 44:6* thus: "This is what the Lord says - Israel's King and Redeemer the Lord Almighty! I am the first and I am the last, apart from me there is no God." In *Psalm 90:2*, it is said, "Before the mountains were born or you brought forth the whole world, from everlasting to everlasting you are God." God initiated human history and Himself is deeply involved in this history (ab initio ad inifitum - Latin for, "from the beginning to eternity.") People are on a journey in life from God to God, where the justified ones will be saved and live eternally. In the Bible God is also known as the God of Abraham, Isaac and Jacob *(Exodus 3:15)*. He is the God of the living people eternally. God provides, guides, protects, advises, warns, encourages, comforts and saves the obedient ones from sin as people travel the life journey to eternity. God is the shepherd as experienced by King David in *Psalm 23:1-6*. In *Genesis 16:13*, Hagar knew God as El Roi meaning God who sees me. God who is omnipresent or in all places sees us everywhere we are. He knows what we think and plan to do.

We cannot hide away from Him. In *Psalm 91:1*, God is known as El Shaddai, meaning God Almighty. It is said, *"Whoever dwells in the shelter of the Most-High will rest in the shadow of the Almighty."* God is invincible - *"Deus Invictus est."* This God is *"I am"* or *"He That Is."* Yahweh or *"Jehovah"* meaning, *"He brings into existence whatever exists."* That is why God is known as the Creator of heaven and earth and He owns them as the Sovereign Ruler *(Deuteronomy 6:4-6)*. There is no one like Him on earth and in heaven hence we should worship Him and Him alone.

God called Abram He later called Abraham from Mesopotamia and made a covenant with him which would also be binding on his posterity who would be a blessing to the nations of the world *(Genesis 12:1-3)*. In this covenant, obedience was required from Abraham and his descendants to be connected to God for them to remain God's chosen people to teach people in the world about the living God and how they could be saved from sin and be His in eternity. When the Israelites, the descendants of Abraham were taken captives in Egypt, they were liberated by God through Moses and were led to the Promised Land of Canaan. At Mount Sinai, gave the Israelites the ten commandments as the covenant to be observed as God's will for them to please Him and for them to be blessed. God guided the Israelites through their leader Moses to cross the Red Sea and the desert where they were provided with food - manna, quails and water for their existence. God protected His people from venomous snakes, hunger, thirst, desert weather and exhaustion till they reached the Promised Land under the leadership of Joshua, after the death of Moses. Their occupation of Canaan was not easy as they met resistance from the Canaanites, the indigenous inhabitants of Cannan. Battles were fought and they were enabled by God to win the battles in order to establish their pieces of settlement.

From time to time, the Israelites violated God's covenant when they got involved in idolatry. God called the prophets in order to remind the people of their need to observe the covenant disobedience or sin was punishable by God who does not want to be worshipped side by side with gods. When the Israelites in the Northern kingdom where the prophets and Hosea worked amongst them insisted to disobey God, they were defeated by the Assyrians in the year 721BC. All the ten tribes of Israel were taken into captivity and they never returned. However, the two tribes of the Israelites then known as the Jews in the Southern kingdom remained as they remained observing the covenant which the prophets there, like Isaiah, Micah and Jeremiah kept on impressing on them to observe to please and avoid the anger of God for their survival. In the event of their disobedience, God could use the nations around them to punish them.

As time went on, during the time of the Prophet Jeremiah, the Jews under King Rehoboam began to act like the other ten tribes in the Northern kingdom who were under King Jeroboam who were captured by the Assyrians. They disobeyed what the prophets of God told them and violated the covenant of God with them. God used a nation more powerful than the Jews themselves as a means of punishing the Jews and these were the Babylonians. Influential Jews were taken into Babylonian captivity. The prophets Ezekiel and Daniel served the fellow Babylonian captives to help them to uphold God's covenant. At the expiry of their period of captivity, the Persians King defeated the Babylonians according to God's plan to liberate the Jews for them to return to Judea in order to resettle there and rebuild the temple of God that had been destroyed by the Babylonians.

God the Father was experienced in many ways in the Old Testament as the Israelites focal point of theocracy even when they chose King Saul as their political leader and commander in times of wars against the nations around them. God remained one too be consulted in times of wars and natural calamities according to their faith. The history of the Hebrews, Israelites or Jews depict the universality of God's rule and leadership among all nations of the world through His grace as people created in His image. In the Old Testament, the Holy Spirit is referred to as the Spirit of God. In *Psalm 143:10*, a mention is made about the Holy Spirit, *"Teach me to do your will. For you are my God: may your good Spirit lead me on level ground."* In *Judges 6:34*, we can see the Holy Spirit involved in the history of the Israelites: *"Then the Spirit of the Lord came on Gideon, and he blew a trumpet, summoning the Abiezrites to follow him."* The verse that follows in *Judges 15:14* reads thus: *"As he approached Lehi, the Philistines came toward him shouting. The Spirit of the Lord came powerfully upon him. The ropes on his arms became like charred flax, and the bindings dropped from his hands."* The other verses that mention the Spirit of God are *2 Samuel 23:2* and *Ezekiel 2:2ᵃ*.

Believers in God and nonbelievers are all under God's care and all of them are urged to acknowledge Him as their Creator for whom they were created in His own image to seek Him and follow Him for His will to be done on earth as it is in heaven. People are expected to worship and serve Him and fellow people in righteousness and justly. All people sin against God in thought, word and deed but blessed are those who are remorseful of their sinfulness and repent in order to be forgiven by God from their sins. Faith in God should be part of the people's life to remain connected to the Creator. In the Old Testament Jesus, the Word of God that was spoken by God in the creation story *(Genesis 1:1-31; 2:1-2)* and things came into existence, became flesh for our sake to save us from sin and eternal death through faith in Him and by God's grace *(John 1:1-4; John 3:16)*.

Jesus Christ the Redeemer of Mankind

The Old Testament based on the law or Torah in Hebrew is the covenant of God with the chosen people of God, the Hebrews which was succeeded by the New Testament the new covenant of God with the people who believe in Him through Jesus Christ. Jesus is the sacrificial Lamb of God who suffered and died vicariously for the sins of all the people on earth. He paid our debt of sin for all the born and unborn people for our salvation *(Colossians 2:13-14)*. Jesus fulfilled the Old Testament in that what was meant to be achieved by the Law in the Old Testament or covenant and the prophets was finally fulfilled by Jesus the sacrificial Lamb of God *"Agnus Dei,"* on the cross as an expiation of our sins for our redemption. This is God's plan.

Jesus is the universal 'Good News' to all the people. Through Him we have the unmerited grace of God hence Christian believers in God enjoy to sing the hymn; "Tis So Sweet To Trust In Jesus."

> Tis so sweet to trust in Jesus
> Just to take Him at His word
> Just to rest upon His promise
> Just to know, "Thus saith the Lord."
>
> Jesus, Jesus, how I trust Him
> How I've proved Him o'er and o'er
> Jesus, Jesus, precious Jesus
> Oh, for grace to trust Him more.
>
> I'm so glad I learned to trust Him
> Precious Jesus, Saviour Friend
> And I know that He is with me
> Will be with me to the end
>
> Jesus, Jesus, how I trust Him
> How I've proved Him o'er and o'er
> Jesus, Jesus, precious Jesus
> Oh, for grace to trust Him more

> Jesus, Jesus, how I trust Him
> How I've proved Him o'er and o'er
> Jesus, Jesus, precious Jesus
> Oh, for grace to trust Him more
> Oh, for grace to trust Him more.
>
> *Songwriters: Canzetta Staton/ Louisa M. Stead; William James.*

The birth of Jesus was announced by a great prophet of the Old Testament in *Isaiah 7:14*. Other references to Jesus in the Old Testament are: *Isaiah 9:2-7; Isaiah 40:3-5; Isaiah 42:1-9.*

In the New Testament Jesus said, "Do not let your hearts be troubled. You believe in God, believe also in me *(John 14:1)*; "I am the way and the truth and the life. No one comes to the Father except through me." *(John 14:6),* "Don't you believe that I am in the Father, and that the Father is in me? The words I say to you I do not speak on my own authority. Rather, it is the Father, living in me, who is doing his work. Believe me when I say that I am in the Father, living in me, or at least believe on the evidence of the works themselves." *(John 14:10-11).* In *John 8:23-29,* Jesus affirms His oneness with God the Father for our salvation.

Jesus was on the divine mission in the world, as prophesied by Isaiah in *Isaiah 61:1-2* which was read by Jesus Christ in the Synagogue in Nazareth, as recorded in *Luke 4:18-19.* What was written by Isaiah alluded to Jesus Christ who fulfilled and affirmed the prophecy in the hearing of the attendees. The mission of God was fulfilled by Jesus in saving mankind through Jesus Himself who taught people about God, Himself and the Holy Spirit, preached about the Kingdom of God and how people can be saved from sin through faith in Him. The climax of Jesus mission was reached when He was crucified and died on the cross as the sacrificial Lamb of God, for the sins of humanity. Jesus' resurrection and appearances to His followers proved that He was truly alive. Sin and death were conquered on behalf of all the people for the debt of sin was paid in full. The mission of Jesus was short but very effective as the church was established as an institution of salvation of people from sin through faith in the Triune God. Jesus' disciples went on proclaiming the Gospel about Jesus Christ which is the good news about our salvation from sin and eternal death, through Jesus Christ Himself and by God's grace *(John 3:16)*, became the faith or religion of the followers of Jesus who were first known as Christians in Antioch *(Acts 11:26)*. These followers of Jesus had been empowered by the Holy Spirit who Jesus promised disciples who later came to be known as apostles, the name formed from the Greek word 'apostelos' meaning a 'messenger' which is derived from the Greek verb 'apostelo' meaning 'I send'. *(John 14:15-17; Acts 1:8; Acts 2:1-13)*. The Holy Spirit would help the followers of Jesus by guiding, counselling, warn about dangers, comfort, empower and remind the Jesus' teachings to remain committed to Jesus.

The visible coming of the Holy Spirit on the Pentecost Day like tongues of fire, empowered the waiting disciples of Jesus. From that time people of the way or the disciples or apostles of Jesus felt the power of the Holy Spirit that made them preach powerfully, perform miracles, heal and establish the Christian congregations or churches under the Lordship of Jesus. The apostles were promised such church activities in *Acts 1:8*, *"But you will receive power when the Holy Spirit comes on you, and you will be my witnesses in Jerusalem, and in all Judea and Samaria, and to the ends of the earth."* The Holy Spirit works as an advocate counsellor and comforter in the church.

The Christian Faith Journey

The Christian faith journey in the Bible is intertwined with secular history because the one who cares for believers and unbelievers is the same God who expects us all to live the righteous life - the life of obedience to Him. Obedience is rewardable whereas disobedience is punishable by God to the extent of being condemnable on the Judgement Day. The leader in human history or life journey is none other than the Triune God, our Creator upon whom we are dependent for our existence. Because of who God is and what He does to us and for us, He deserves to be worshipped as it is stated in the first greatest commandment *in Matthew 22:37-38, "Love the Lord your God with all your heart and with all your soul and with all your mind. This is the first and greatest commandment."* The second greatest commandment like the first one is, *"Love your neighbour as yourself. All the Law and the prophets hang on these two commandments." (Matthew 22:39-40).* Any violation of one of them discredits one's faith in God. The two commandments summarise the Christian faith and living the life of Christian worship that pleases God, our Lord and the Sovereign Ruler of the universe. It is very important for people to remember what Jesus did for our salvation from sin. This makes us emulate to live a righteous life Paul talking about Jesus says in *Ephesians 1:7-10, "In him we have redemption through his blood, the forgiveness of sins, in accordance with the riches of God's grace that he lavished on us. With all wisdom and understanding, he made known to us mystery of his will according to his good pleasure, which he purposed in Christ, to be put into effect when the times reach their fulfilment - to bring unity to all things in heaven and on earth under Christ."* Those who choose the life of worship will feel greatly encouraged to be told or reminded of what God has done for us in Jesus as expressed in *Hebrews 9:14-15, "How much more, then, will the blood of Christ, who through the eternal Spirit offered himself unblemished to God, cleanse our consciences from acts that lead to death, so that we may serve the living God."* For this reason Christ is the mediator of the new covenant, that those who are called may receive the promised eternal inheritance - now that he has died as a ransom to set free from the sins committed under the first covenant.

The composer of the hymn, *"Are you washed in the blood?"* has many questions that make us introspect as we hope to inherit eternal life. Life on earth is time to be enjoyed in obedience to God to please God Himself and the people in our righteousness. It is time to prepare ourselves for eternity with the Lord. Here is a hymn to be reflected upon as we live in hope for eternal life hereafter:

Are You Washed in the Blood?

Have you been to Jesus for the cleansing power?
Are you washed in the blood of the Lamb?
Are you fully trusted in His grace this hour?
Are you washed in the blood of the Lamb?

Refrain

Are you washed in the blood
In the soul cleansing blood of the Lamb?
Are your garments spotless?
Are they white as snow?
Are you washed in the blood of the Lamb?

Are you walking daily by the Saviour's side?
Are you washed in the blood of the Lamb?
Do you rest each moment in the crucified?
Are you washed in the blood of the Lamb?

Refrain

Are you washed in the blood
In the soul cleansing blood of the Lamb?
Are your garments spotless?
Are they white as snow?
Are you washed in the blood of the Lamb?

> When the bridegroom cometh will your robes be white?
> Are you washed in the blood of the lamb?
> Will your soul be ready for the mansions bright,
> And be washed in the blood of the Lamb?
>
> *Refrain*
>
> Are you washed in the blood
> In the soul cleansing blood of the Lamb?
> Are your garments spotless?
> Are they white as snow?
> Are you washed in the blood of the Lamb?
>
> Lay aside the garments that are stained with sin.
> And be washed in the blood of the Lamb;
> There's fountain flowing for the soul unclean,
> O be washed in the blood of the Lamb!
>
> *Refrain*
>
> Are you washed in the blood
> In the soul cleansing blood of the Lamb?
> Are your garments spotless?
> Are they white as snow?
> Are you washed in the blood of the Lamb?

In conclusion, we are what we are in the journey of faith by choice that is based on predestination. God foresaw our faith journey before we were born whether we would accept Him or not and by His grace we were born on earth. He does not force us to follow Him but He reveals Himself to all people through general revelation - the created things and conscience and specific revelation in Jesus Christ His only begotten Son. The choice to follow or not is ours. God loves all people but He hates their abominations. He wants people to reciprocate their love to Him who loved them first through His creation and redemption through Jesus Christ on the cross.

In *Hebrews 9:28*, we read, *"So Christ was sacrificed once to take away the sins of many; and he will appear a second time, not to bear sin, but to bring salvation to those who are waiting for him."* We, people created in God's image, are expected to do His will to be saved from sin. In *1 John 1:7*, it is said, *"But if we walk in the light, as he is in the light, we have fellowship with one another, and the blood of Jesus, his Son, purifies us from all sin."* This is why we have to live the life of worship for that is to wait for the Saviour who is coming at the end of the known time, to reward those who adhered to their faith in Him as stated in *Revelation 22:12*, *"Look, I am coming soon! My reward is with me and I will give to each person according to what they have done."* The word of God expresses the convincing truth that leads to our salvation from sin and eternal death. If only we can be humble before God and accept His word gratefully, we can be transformed by the renewing of our mind. *(Romans 12:2)*.

Children of God by adoption have been given a great responsibility by our Lord Jesus, of winning the souls of the people for Jesus Christ Himself through the propagation of the word of God and deeds acceptable to God Himself. The writer urges the Christian believers to announce the presence of the Holy Spirit among ourselves to guide and comfort us always until the end of time. The Holy Spirit dwells within our hearts *(John 14:15-17)*. Here is one hymn that revives the souls of the soldiers of the cross:

The comforter has come

O spread the tidings 'round
Whenever man is found,
Wherever human hearts and human woes abound,
Let every Christian tongue proclaim the joyful sound
The Comforter has come!

Refrain

The comforter has come, the comforter has come!
The Holy Ghost from heaven, the Father's promise
Given;
O spread the tidings wherever man is found;
The comforter has come!

The long, long night is past, the morning breaks
At last,
And hushed the dreadful wail and fury of the blast,
As o'er the golden hills the day advances fast!
The comforter has come!

Refrain

The comforter has come, the comforter has come!
The Holy Ghost from heaven, the Father's promise
Given;
O spread the tidings wherever man is found;
The comforter has come!

Lo, the great King of kings with healing in His wings,
To every captive soul a full deliverance brings;
And through the vacant calls the song of
Triumph rings;
The comforter has come!

Refrain

The comforter has come, the comforter has come!
The Holy Ghost from heaven, the Father's promise
Given;
O spread the tidings wherever man is found;
The comforter has come!

O boundless love divine! How shall this tongue of Mine,
To wondering mortals tell the matchless grace divine:
That I, a child of hell, should in His image shine!
The comforter has come!

Refrain

The comforter has come, the comforter has come!
The Holy Ghost from heaven, the Father's promise Given;
O spread the tidings wherever man is found;
The comforter has come!

Source: African Methodist Episcopal Church Hymnal #199

Living the life of worship makes the worshippers enjoy the fellowship with God our Maker by whom we were created in His image and for whom we are. Through the prevenient grace of God, people come to know that Jesus is Lord *(Romans 10:9; 1 Corinthians 12:3)* and become children of God *(John 1:12-13)* by God's justifying grace followed by sanctifying grace.

References

The NIV Bible
1. Ngoma Dze United Methodist Church Ye Zimbabwe
2. An African American ecumenical hymnal
3. Faith Publishing House Evening Light songs
4. Baptism Hymnal
5. African Methodist Episcopal Church Hymnal

www.ingramcontent.com/pod-product-compliance
Lightning Source LLC
Chambersburg PA
CBHW061211070526
44583CB00025B/3203